Forever
BEATLES

Forever BEATLES

John Alvarez Taylor

SMITHMARK

This edition published in 1992 by SMITHMARK Publishers Inc., 112 Madison Avenue New York, New York 10016

SMITHMARK books are available for bulk purchase for sales promotion and premium use. For details write or telephone the Manager of Special Sales, SMITHMARK Publishers Inc., 112 Madison Avenue, New York, NY 10016. (212) 532-6600.

Produced by Brompton Books Corp., 15 Sherwood Place Greenwich, CT 06830

ISBN 0-8317-3468-X

Printed in Hong Kong

10 9 8 7 6 5 4 3 2 1

All photos are from the AGS Picture Archives with these exceptions: © Pictorial Press 39, 50 (top), 63

Page 1: Paul, George, Ringo and John in the opening scene from their 1965 United Artists motion picture, *Help!*
Page 2: The Beatles in 1967, at the time of their epochal album *Sgt Pepper's Lonely Heart's Club Band* — released on the Parlophone label in the UK, and on the Capitol Records label in the US.
These pages: On the set of *A Hard Day's Night*, a 1964 United Artists motion picture.

CONTENTS

INTRODUCTION

They were 'four lads from Liverpool' who changed pop music forever. They were The Beatles—also known as John Lennon, Paul McCartney, George Harrison and Ringo Starr.

Because of its status as a major saltwater port, Liverpool was one of the first cities in the British Isles to hear of that 1950s American phenomenon, rock 'n roll. Therefore, Liverpool was a hotbed of early British rock 'n roll 'skiffle groups.'

One of the premier 'skiffle group' leaders, John Lennon, was born on 9 October 1940 to Alfred and Julia Lennon. In 1956, he started his first band, calling it the Quarrymen for an area of Liverpool.

That same year, John enlisted talented young left-handed guitarist James Paul McCartney, better known as 'Paul,' born on 18 June 1942. Then, in 1958, gangly young George Harrison, born on 25 February 1943, joined the band.

At this point, Stuart Sutcliffe played bass and Thomas Moore played drums for the Quarrymen. The Quarrymen disbanded in November of 1959. The band reformed in 1960, with a new name—'Silver Beatles.' This band crossed the Channel for gigs in Hamburg, a center of the European youth scene.

Pete Best took over as drummer, and The Silver Beatles were invited to play backup for Tony Sheridan for recording sessions in Hamburg. Their first single, 'My Bonnie Lies Over the Ocean,' backed with 'The Saints (Go Marchin' In),' resulted from these sessions. Stuart Sutcliffe stayed in Hamburg when the group decided to return home.

Back in Liverpool, the Silver Beatles were becoming a real phenomenon. Brian Epstein, manager of North England Music Stores Ltd (NEMS), was intrigued by this young band, and talked his way into becoming their manager. At his behest, they replaced drummer Pete Best with Richard Starkey—better known as Ringo Starr, born on 7 July 1940.

By the end of July, 1962, Epstein had orchestrated a groundswell of support for the group, which was now known as The Beatles. EMI Records was persuaded to sign The Beatles to its Parlophone label. Later, a deal was worked out whereby the band's American distributor would be Capitol Records—and later, of course,

Apple Records would come into the picture, with complications all its own.

On 11 September 1962, The Beatles recorded their first single, 'Love Me Do,' backed with 'PS I Love You.' The Beatles, brilliantly managed by Brian Epstein, were on their way.

Over the years, they collectively starred in the motion pictures *A Hard Day's Night* (United Artists, 1964) and *Help!* (United Artists, 1965), as well as the television special *Magical Mystery Tour* (BBC-TV, 1967). Their documentaries included *Let It Be* (Apple Films, 1970), and they even lent their voices to an animated feature, *Yellow Submarine* (King Features, 1968).

The following is a list of Beatles albums, excluding 'greatest hits,' and other such compilations: *Please Please Me* (Parlophone/Capitol of Canada, 1963); *Introducing the Beatles* (VeeJay 1963); *With the Beatles/Beatlemania With the Beatles* (Parlophone/Capitol of Canada, 1963); *Meet the Beatles!* (Capitol, 1964); *The Beatles' Second Album* (Capitol, 1964); *Long Tall Sally* (Capitol of Canada, 1964); *The Beatles' First* (Polydor, 1964); *A Hard Day's Night* (United Artists, 1964); *Something New* (Capitol, 1964); *The Beatles Story* (Capitol, 1964); *Beatles for Sale* (Parlophone, 1964); *Beatles '65* (Capitol, 1964); *The Early Beatles* (Capitol, 1965); *Beatles VI* (Capitol, 1965); *Help!* (Parlophone, 1965); *Help!/Soundtrack Album* (Capitol, 1965); *Rubber Soul* (Parlophone/Capitol, 1965); *Yesterday and Today* (Capitol, 1966); *Revolver* (Parlophone/Capitol, 1966); *Sgt Pepper's Lonely Hearts Club Band* (Parlophone/Capitol, 1967); *Magical Mystery Tour* (Capitol, 1967); *The Beatles* (Apple/Parlophone/Capitol, 1968); *Yellow Submarine* (Apple/Parlophone/Capitol, 1969); *Abbey Road* (Apple/Parlophone/Capitol, 1969/78); *Let It Be* (Apple/Parlophone/Capitol, 1970).

With their breakup at the turn of the decade, The Beatles went off to work on individual projects. Together, they were the most important rock 'n roll band of the 1960s, and separated, they continued to influence the pop scene in interesting ways.

Facing page: The Beatles in 1965, the year of the album *Rubber Soul*, which hinted at new horizons for them. *Rubber Soul* was released on the Parlophone label in the UK, and on the Capitol Records label in the US.

Early Years

Above: The Beatles posing in Hamburg in 1961, where they played often in the very early 1960s. Pete Best (at photo left) was then the band's drummer.

Facing page: George Harrison, Paul McCartney and John Lennon on stage at the Cavern Club in Liverpool, circa 1962.

That they were a 'hot' band even then is evidenced by the January, 1962 *Mersey Beat* headline *at right*.

Hamburg Days

In 1961–62, the thing to do was to cross the Channel to play in Hamburg, which was the center of the West German youth scene.

During the band's 'Hamburg days,' circa 1961: John Lennon, at *left*, and George Harrison, *facing page*.

Richard Starkey, alias Ringo Starr, became The Beatles' drummer in August, 1962. *Above:* Paul, George, John and Ringo in 1962.

Love Me Do

The Beatles' first bona fide hit, 'Love Me Do,' hit the charts in the winter of 1962–63. After that, their popularity exploded.

These pages: At Brian Epstein's behest, they donned the suits and sported the 'mop-top' haircuts that would identify them for their fans.

In 1963, they released several albums in the UK, the US and Canada, including *Please Please Me*, *Introducing the Beatles* and *With the Beatles*.

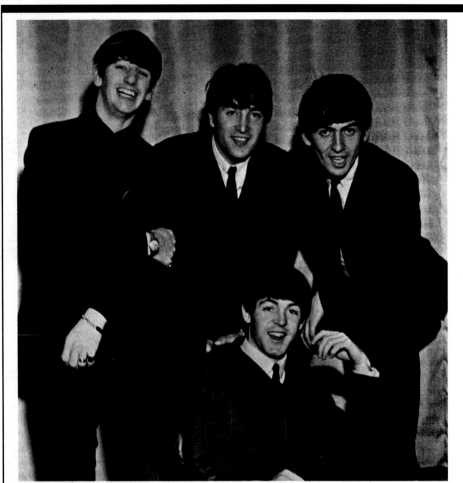

Beatlemania

Below and facing page: The Beatles in the Royal Variety Performance at the Prince of Wales Theatre, on 4 November 1963. The sounds of John, Paul, George and Ringo were by then ringing throughout England. The British press coined the term 'Beatlemania' in October 1963.

As of December of that year, five Beatles singles were in the UK Top 20, and the albums *With the Beatles* and *Please Please Me* were first and second on the album charts.

They were affectionately known as the 'Fab Four,' and wherever they went, they were mobbed by crowds of fans. Even so, they had yet to have their effect on the US. *At left:* The Beatles in 1963.

The Ed Sullivan Show

Above: The Beatles wave hello to the US at Kennedy Airport in New York City on 7 February 1964.

They came to the US for two appearances on CBS Television's *Ed Sullivan Show*, plus concerts in Washington, DC, Miami and New York's prestigious Carnegie Hall.

Facing page: The Beatles in concert on the *Ed Sullivan Show*. *At left:* The Fab Four with their American television host, Ed Sullivan.

The Coming Thing

Facing page: The Beatles and the set that was constructed for one of their *Ed Sullivan Show* concerts. This set had a futuristic style that proclaimed The Beatles as 'the coming thing.' *At right:* A closeup of George Harrison.

Ed Sullivan's sober expression *(below)* belied the enthusiasm of American fans. In fact, the band's playing was rendered all but inaudible by the enthusiastic screams of their audience.

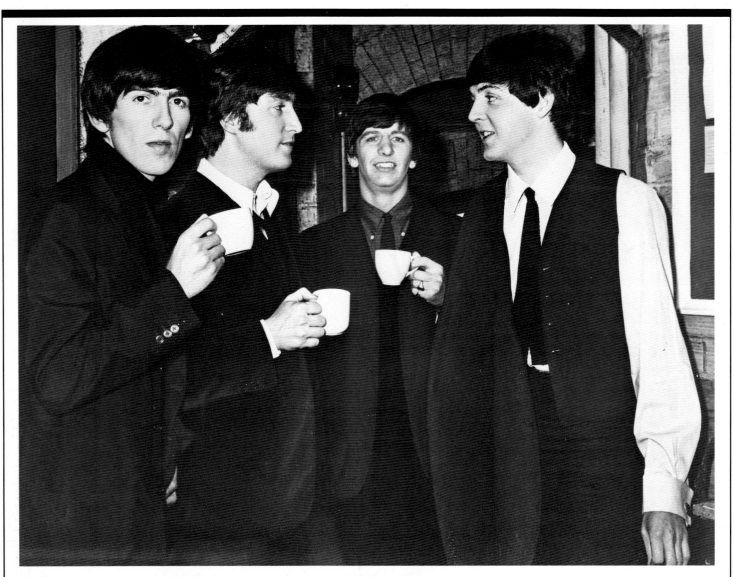

A Hard Day's Night

The Beatles began work on their first feature film, *A Hard Day's Night*, on 2 March 1964. It was conceived as a highly whimsical portrait of their lives on the road. *Above:* A publicity still for *A Hard Day's Night*.

While *A Hard Day's Night* was in production, Parlophone and Capitol released a half dozen singles in the UK and the US, producing five Beatles hits in the US Top 10, and dominance in the singles, album and sheet music listings in the UK.

Facing page and at left: Paul and Ringo, respectively, on the set of *A Hard Day's Night*.

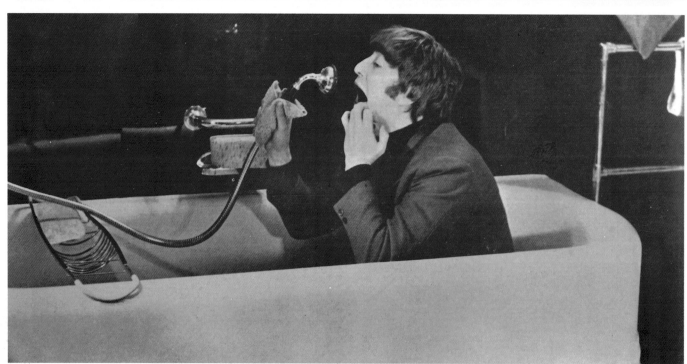

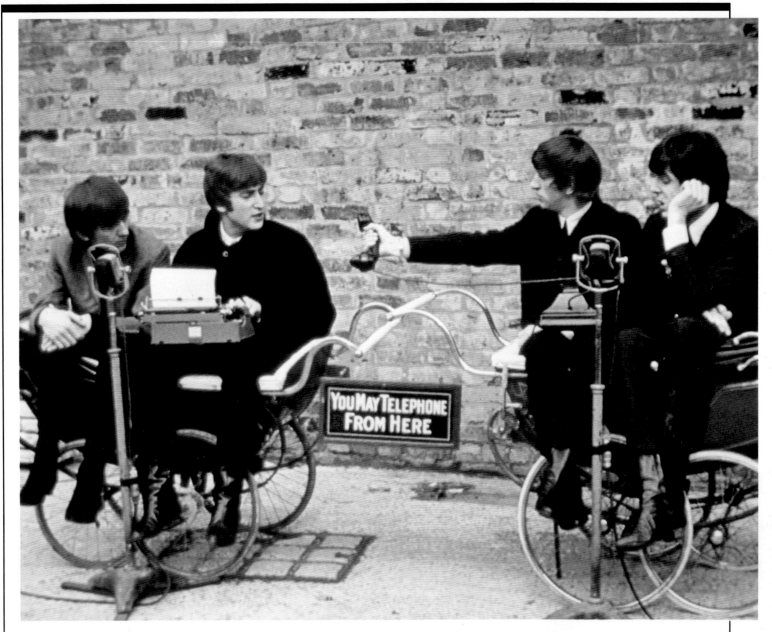

A Hard Day Continued

Above left: Director Richard Lester, George Harrison, Ringo Starr and John Lennon on location in London for *A Hard Day's Night*.

Some of the film's many light moments: John Lennon *(at left)* in a moment of do-it-yourself dental hygiene; and The Beatles *(above)* demonstrate the concept of a 'movable office.'

At right: George takes a break during the filming of *A Hard Day's Night*.

Day's End

John Lennon compiled his humorous book, *In His Own Write*, during the filming of *A Hard Day's Night*. The book was published on 23 March 1964, and immediately won the Foyle's Literary Prize.

These pages, at top: High moments in a *Hard Day's Night*. *At left:* A promotional still of 'those four lads from Liverpool,' for *A Hard Day's Night*.

At right: The Beatles with their legendary manager, Brian Epstein, and Great Britain's Princess Margaret. This photo was taken at the world premier of *A Hard Day's Night* on 6 July 1964.

The film was a smash hit, and both the title single and the sound track album hit Number One on American and British charts within a month of the film's release.

Live Beatles

Previous pages: Taking a break on their US tour. *Facing page:* In live performance on the UK's *Ready, Steady, Go!* television show.

On 19 August 1964, they began their first full-fledged American tour in San Francisco, moving on to Las Vegas, Seattle, Vancouver, Los Angeles, Denver, Cincinnati, New York City, Atlantic City, Indianapolis, Milwaukee, Chicago, Detroit, Toronto, Montreal, Jacksonville, Boston, Baltimore, Pittsburgh, Cleveland, New Orleans, Kansas City, Dallas and back again to New York City, to complete the tour on 20 September 1964.

This page: In live concert. Their hairstyles and brashness caused a sensation in the US. Heavy resistance was offered by fans of Elvis Presley-style 'rockabilly' music, but The Beatles won the day.

Help!

On 22 February 1965, The Beatles began their second motion picture, *Help!* An entertainingly silly film, it featured oddball suspense and the whimsical humor that had succeeded in *A Hard Day's Night*. *Facing page:* On location in the Bahamas. *Above and at right:* The Beatles in scenes from *Help!*

Help! premiered successfully on 29 July 1965. The single and the albums (see the album list in our Introduction) became Number One in the US and the UK.

On The Road

On 12 June 1965, Queen Elizabeth had made John, Paul, George and Ringo members of the Most Excellent Order of the British Empire.

Thus, they became the most *distinguished* rock 'n roll group ever to tour the UK, Europe or America.

This page: The Beatles during their 1966 American tour. *Facing page:* Views of a 1966 press conference.

The Last Tour

One 23 June 1966, The Beatles left London for Munich, Germany, for their last world tour.

By that time, the *Help!* album was joined by the epochal *Rubber Soul* album in Top 10 charts world wide.

The tour would include, as it had in other years, the UK, Europe and America, and this year included the Far East. After that tour, The Beatles spent most of their time as a group in EMI's Abbey Road and St John's Wood studios, where they were given virtually free rein.

These pages: Scenes from the last Beatles tour ever to occur.

Studio Time

When they performed their last concert—in San Francisco, on 29 August 1966—it was not the last of The Beatles, but part of a new phase. Intensive work in the studio produced nuances that would be drowned out by the screaming fans at a typical Beatles concert.

The first album done in this mode had been *Rubber Soul*, and the second, which really confirmed their new direction, was *Revolver*, released on 5 August 1966.

Above: John and George in the studio for the recording of *Revolver*. *At left:* Posing in the Abbey Road studios. *Facing page:* The Beatles in late 1966.

Sgt Pepper

Facing page: The much-changed Beatles pose with their classic album, *Sgt Pepper's Lonely Hearts Club Band.* This album truly buried the 'old' Beatles—though echoes would remain in the band's songs.

An eclectic mix of songs unified by a psychedelic sensibility, *Sgt Pepper*— as it was popularly known—heralded the 'new' Beatles.

The Beatles were on the leading edge of a wave of change that was sweeping the popular music world— and it was a tidal wave. *Sgt Pepper's*

Lonely Hearts Club Band not only was a milestone for the Beatles, but it also became a symbol of 1967—the year the tidal wave struck—a year which itself is regarded as a landmark in popular music history. Twenty years later, the 'sixties' are still seen as a mother lode of important popular music, which begat an unprecedented explosion of creative output that was felt in every corner of the globe.

The album's recording was finished on 30 March 1967 and it was released on 1 June 1967. *Above:* 'Sgt Pepper's Lonely Hearts Club Band' at the Saville Theatre, filming a promotional film for the album.

Mystery Tour

At left: Paul, Ringo, John and George in EMI's Abbey Road studios, where they recorded the songs for yet another major effort in 1967—the fragmentary film, *Magical Mystery Tour.*

Below: Paul, as Major McCartney with his aide Sergeant Spinelli, in the recruiting office sequence from the film.

Magic Alone

At 54 minutes, it was too short to be a feature film, so *Magical Mystery Tour*, though shot in color, premiered in black-and-white on BBC-TV, on 26 December 1967.

Although the television show was panned by critics, the soundtrack album—released on 8 December 1967—attained Gold Record status by 15 December 1967.

Highlights. *At right:* Ringo and Paul as two of the magicians whose incantation begins the 'tour.' *Below:* The band, performing 'Iam the Walrus,' backed by a chorus of 'Eggmen' at West Malling RAF base.

Yellow Submarine

Shortly after The Beatles' brilliant manager, Brian Epstein, died on 27 August 1967, they formed their own media company, and called it Apple Corps Ltd.

One of the first projects to be initiated by the new company was the completion of an all-animated feature film based on The Beatles' 1966 hit song, 'Yellow Submarine.'

Actually begun in 1967, *Yellow Submarine* premiered in the UK on 17 July 1968, and in the US on 13 November 1968. Baffled reviewers used the terms 'indescribable,' 'stupendous,' 'friendly' and 'cute' to describe the film.

At left and below: Stills from *Yellow Submarine*. *At right:* The Beatles with their yellow submarine. *Below left:* A celebratory image, but what did the future hold?

The Future

John had first met the Japanese artist Yoko Ono in 1966, but they did not become romantically involved until 1968. *Below:* John and Yoko at a gallery opening in 1968.

Yoko was said to be taking John away from The Beatles, but the band had been apart more than together since they'd stopped touring two years before, and work with other performers was much a part of The Beatles' lives at that point. *Facing page:* John with Eric Clapton, playing 'Yer Blues' for the unreleased motion picture *Rock 'n Roll Circus*.

Paul *(at left)* also found a lasting partner in 1968: Linda Eastman, whom he would marry.

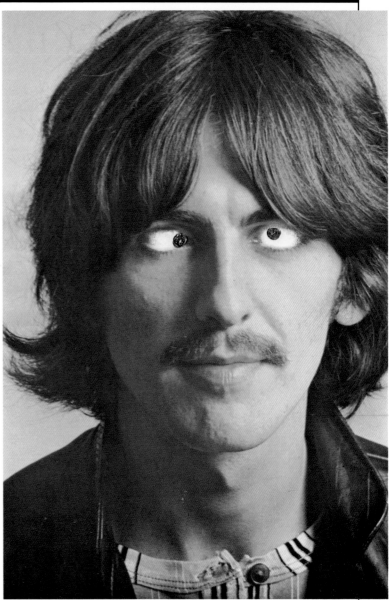

The White Album

This four-sided album was The Beatles' *magnum opus* and included 'Back in the USSR,' 'Julia,' 'Yer Blues,' 'While My Guitar Gently Weeps,' 'I Will,' 'Revolution,' 'Blackbird' and other great songs.

Officially named *The Beatles*, its all-white cover inspired its more popular, unofficial title: 'The White Album.' Released in the UK on 22 November and in the US on 25 November 1968, it became Number One on the *Melody Maker* charts and was affirmed as a Gold Record in the US by the first week of December.

Above, both pages: The Beatles of 'The White Album.' *At left:* Side one. *At right:* On the street in 1968.

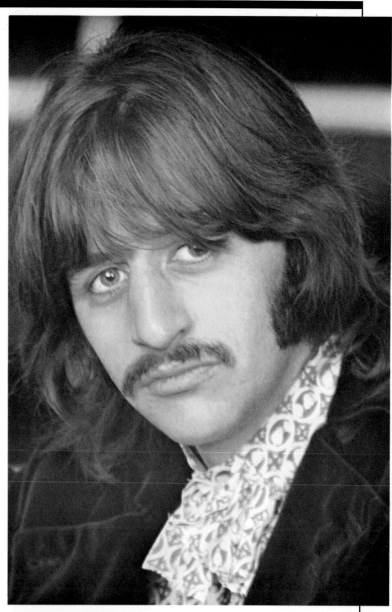

Let It Be

As a band, they were rapidly unravelling. Apple Corps Ltd was also coming apart.

On 2 January 1969, The Beatles began filming a documentary of themselves making an album. By 30 January, over 100 songs (mostly old standards, with approximately 12 Lennon and McCartney songs) had been recorded, and 28 hours of session work had been filmed. The sessions ended with The Beatles' last live concert, atop Apple headquarters, on 30 January 1969.

The *Get Back* album was released in August, 1969, withdrawn, rearranged and re-titled *Let It Be*, on 8 May 1970. The film, *Let It Be*, was released in May 1970.

These pages: The Beatles during the *Get Back/Let It Be* sessions.

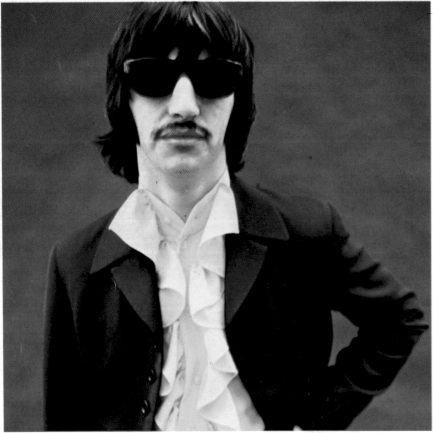

Apple Corps

The Beatles had spent their adult lives being managed by Brian Epstein. So, when they somewhat quixotically formed their own management and production company, Apple Corps Ltd (see also text, page 43), they soon discovered that they knew nothing of business.

After a request by George to dissolve the partnership, a tax writ against Apple Corps by the British government and a suit against the other three Beatles by Paul—all in late 1970—Apple Corps Ltd would essentially cease to exist.

These pages: A Beatles photo session in 1969, when Apple Corps Ltd was still viable.

Abbey Road

The *Abbey Road* album was recorded at EMI's Abbey Road studios. It was released in September and October of 1969 in the UK and the US respectively, riding the *Billboard* charts for 87 weeks. *Facing page:* The Beatles at the time of *Abbey Road*. *At right:* John in the studio.

'Oh! Darling,' 'Come Together,' 'Something' and 'Octopus's Garden' added to its brilliant complexity of material—as did the medley and fragment that ended Side Two.

It was the last time The Beatles would be together in a studio. After the final mix on 20 August 1969, they went their separate ways.

Starr

Ringo's post-Beatle albums have included *Sentimental Journey* and *Beaucoups of Blues* (both 1970); *Ringo* (1973); *Goodnight Vienna* (1974); *Blast From Your Past* (1975); *Ringo's Rotogravure* (1976); *Ringo the Fourth* and *Scouse the Mouse/Soundtrack Album* (both 1977); *Bad Boy* (1978); and *Stop and Smell the Roses* (1981).

At left: With Shelley Long in *Caveman* (1981). *At far left:* In *The Magic Christian* (1970). *Below left:* In *That'll Be the Day* (1972). *Below:* His wedding with Barbara Bach. *Above:* Ringo in 1974.

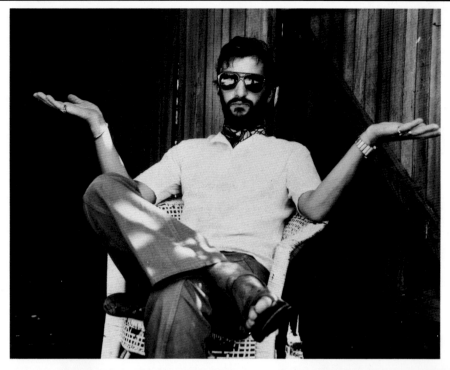

Harrison

George Harrison's post-Beatle albums include *All Things Must Pass* (1970); *Concert for Bangla Desh* (with Ravi Shankar, Bob Dylan and others, 1971/72); *Living in the Material World* (1973); *Dark Horse* (1974); *Extra Texture* (1975); *The Best of George Harrison* and *Thirty-Three and a Third* (both 1976); *George Harrison* (1979); *Somewhere in England* (1981); *Gone Troppo* (1982); and *Cloud Nine* (1988).

Facing page: During the Concert for Bangla Desh. *Above:* An album photo for *All Things Must Pass*. *At right:* George Harrison.

McCartney

Paul McCartney's post-Beatles efforts include leading a band named Wings from 1971–78.

His albums include: *McCartney* (1970); *Ram* and *Wild Life* (both 1971); *Red Rose Speedway* and *Band on the Run* (both 1973); *Venus and Mars* (1975); *Wings at the Speed of Sound* and *Wings Over America* (both 1976); *London Town* and *Wings' Greatest* (both 1978); *Back to the Egg* (1979); *McCartney II* (1980); *Tug of War* (1982); *Pipes of Peace* (1983); *Give My Regards to Broad Street* (1984); and *All the Best* (1988).

He also produced and starred in a motion picture, *Give My Regards to Broad Street* (1984), and lately has engaged in such exploits as 'The Paul McCartney World Tour' of 1990. *Above:* Paul and Linda McCartney. *At left:* Paul and a younger McCartney. *Facing page:* Paul McCartney during his 1990 tour.

Lennon

John's post-Beatles albums include: *Unfinished Music I* (1968); *Unfinished Music II*, *Wedding Album* and *Live Peace in Toronto* (all 1969); *John Lennon* (1970); *Imagine* (1971); *Sometime in New York City* (1972); *Mind Games* (1973); *Walls and Bridges* (1974); *Rock 'n Roll* and *Shaved Fish* (both 1975); *Double Fantasy* (1980).

John and his wife Yoko Ono did numerous musical and artistic collaborations. He was assassinated on 8 December 1980.

At left: John and Yoko in 1969. *Below:* John in 1974. *Facing page:* John and Yoko in 1980.

Times Past

Below: The Beatles, circa 1963, when Beatlemania erupted full force, and teenagers everywhere emulated the 'collarless' look of The Beatles' distinctive coats.

Facing page: The Beatles, circa 1967. They no longer resembled the 'cute mop-tops' they had been, and were breaking new ground.

Their fans may prefer one of these images over another but, surely, The Beatles' magic is there in each.

They were,in the words of John Lennon, 'The Greatest Show On Earth.' They were the biggest concert draw of their time; they were the most important and popular musical phenomenon in this century. Their records outsold all their competitors during the 1960s. Twenty years after they stopped recording, their recordings still outsell the works of many current bands.

Their music and lyrics changed the lives of that generation—and the generation that followed. Twenty years later, another generation—people too young to ever have had a chance to hear them live—draws both pleasure and inspiration from their music.

The Beatles were simply 'four lads from Liverpool' who came together by chance to form an alchemical reaction that could be seen, heard and felt, yet could not be fully understood.